Good Things To Know

About Gliding on Snow

By Stu Campbell and Tim Petrick

Photographs by Tom Lippert

A SKi Magazine Book

MOUNTAIN SPORTS PRESS • BOULDER, COLORADO

ISBN 0-9676747-0-0

Library of Congress Cataloging-in Publication Data applied for.

Printed in China

Mountain Sports Press
929 Pearl Street, Suite 200
Boulder, Colorado 80302
303-448-7663
email: mtnsportspress@skinet.com

To purchase additional copies of this book, contact us at
mtnsportspress@skinet.com

Table of Contents

This book is

dedicated to gravity,

every snow

glider's friend.

Thanks for the ride.

**Look us up on the Web at
www.boothcreek.com**

Sequences demonstrated by:

Kevin Mitchell
Northstar-at-Tahoe
snow sports guide

Rachel Newton
Northstar-at-Tahoe
snow sports guide

Mike Rogan
Professional Ski Instructors
of America, Alpine
Demonstration Team

As small as it is, this book required a lengthy gestation period. It was born out of our growing concern for the current state of snow sports in the U.S. Despite the rapid growth of snowboarding in recent years, the overall number of people active in snow sports has been declining slightly. Clearly, ski resorts are not giving their guests what they want, particularly when it comes to instruction.

To address this problem we began experimenting with alternative devices for gliding on snow. That process caused us to wonder if there weren't elements common to all snow gliding, no matter what device you use. In the fall of 1998, we met with a group of Booth Creek Resorts snow sports directors at Loon Mountain, New Hampshire: Jeb Boyd of Loon, Johanna Hall from The Summit near Seattle, and Peter Weber of Waterville Valley, New Hampshire. These three individuals helped provide the foundation for this book, and, as the project continued, they contributed invaluable assistance to us.

Snow sports instruction clearly needed streamlining and simplification. Our task became one of distilling 50 years of accumulated knowledge about how people learn to glide down snowy mountains on toys without brakes. Nuggets of truth emerged, which we eventually dubbed Good Things to Know.

These nuggets have withstood the scrutiny of the directors at all of the other Booth Creek Resorts. They have been hammered on, reshaped, rejected, reconsidered, and tested on snow. Each nugget holds meaning beyond its surface statement. Like the paradoxes known as koans that Zen Buddhist monks meditate on to liberate them from the bonds of logical thinking, these Good Things to Know are intended to liberate you from any self-imposed limitations you might have about your ability to have fun on snow-covered mountains. They are meant to be meditated on.

Our heartfelt thanks to all the snow sports directors of all the Booth Creek resorts. You are the real authors of this book.

— **Stu Campbell and Tim Petrick**

Gliding on snow is a dance with gravity. Flight without wings. A sensual, mystical experience. A potentially lifelong addiction. Fortunately, getting hooked on snow-gliding sports is just about the best thing you can do for yourself. It's all about a world of freedom, friendship, and self-expression.

Good Things to Know About Gliding on Snow offers keys to this kingdom.

This gliding world is not about sliding mindlessly down a hill on the slippery soles of your shoes, a rubber tube, a plastic saucer, or a primitive toboggan. With these devices you are at the mercy of gravity, with little control over where you go or how fast you get there. While all those activities are fun, they are profoundly different from the gliding sports we'll discuss in this book.

Controlled gliding is done on carefully engineered devices with edges—called snow toys. Snow toys include snowboards, skis, skiboards, Snowbikes, Ski Foxes, and Snowscoots. Each of these tools has long, flexible steel edges incorporated into their design. In a very real sense, snow toys are cutting tools. Their edges are meant to slice snow, not chop or hack at it. These sharpened corners are your connection to the mountain, "where the rubber meets the road."

Putting this rubber on the road is what this book is all about. In the first section, we explore the fundamentals that apply to all snow toys. Whether you've never experienced the joy of gliding down a snow-covered mountain, or you're a world-class expert capable of carving lines down the steepest slopes, these universal Good Things to Know are the keys to staying upright, avoiding obstacles, and controlling your descent. Most of all, they are the things you need to know to have more fun on the mountain.

In the next sections, we build upon these universal concepts and take a look at a few of the specific Good Things to Know that apply to the primary snow toys in use at resorts around the world. It is important to understand that these individual nuggets, as well as the universal ones mentioned previously, are just the tip of the iceberg. Each Good Thing to Know can be explored for a lifetime as you improve your skills at riding the various snow toys. Although this book will get you started in the right direction, you will progress faster if you get on-snow help—from friends who have the expertise to assist you, or, better yet, professional coaches or instructors.

On the surface, the advice in this book may seem very simple. Don't be fooled. You can probably read the entire book in perhaps 20 minutes, but you could spend the next 20 years absorbing what it all means. Gliding on snow is an endless feast of possibilities. As you improve, you'll be able to go wherever you want on the mountain, as fast or slow as you please, controlling your speed with your edges by drawing curves, back and forth across snowy hills.

Welcome to the winter dance.

Chapter 1

Universal Good Things to Know About Gliding on Snow

All snow toys have curved edges that can bend and grip. If you ride the edge, it will redirect you on a curved downhill route. Use those curved edges to trace curves in the snow, control speed, and go where you want.

There are universal truths about gliding on snow that apply to all snow toys. What works for one works for all. Each Good Thing to Know in this chapter applies to any snow toy you choose, whether skis, a snowboard, skiboards, Snowbike, Ski Fox, or Snowscoot. If a photo shows a snow toy other than the one you use, look at it anyway.

Each page in this chapter shows a universal key to success. Start out with this basic thought:

Gliding on snow is about going from one curve to the next. Don't think about the curve you are in. Think about the curve that's coming up.

The route downhill is always curved. There are no straight lines when you glide on edge.

What's going on here?

To glide on edge you simply tilt or roll the snow toy off its flat base (which simply wants to slide straight) and onto its corner or edge (which wants to make a curve). When you do this, the edge will draw you through a curving path.

Curve uphill to a stop.

What's going on here?

If you keep any snow toy on its edge long enough—staying with the curve—you will glide back up the hill, slow down, and eventually come to a stop.

Slow down by **S**curving uphill;

What's going on here?

Understanding
this simple Good Thing
to Know is as important for the
first-day snow glider as for some-
one trying to control his or her
speed on a very steep slope.
There are no brakes on any snow
toy. You must control its path
down the hill.

speed up by
curving downhill.

Don't turn the edge...

What's going on here?

Trying to turn or twist the
snow toy to change
direction does not work
well. Abrupt movements
tend to throw
you out of balance
and make it hard to
maintain control.

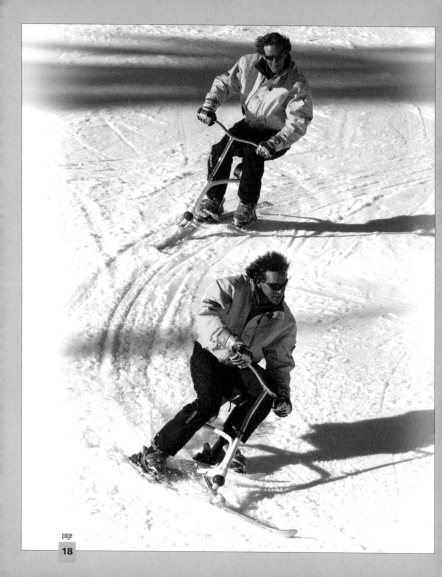

Make the edge turn you.

What's going on here?

Instead, tilt the snow toy on its edge, and the edge will turn you. It is much easier and results in smooth, controlled curves down the slope.

Look where you want to go next.

What's going on here?

Just as a car tends to go where the driver is looking, so will any snow toy.

Change edges to change direction.

What's going on here?

Edge change means going from one gliding edge to the other gliding edge. To curve left, you tilt the snow toy on its left edge. To curve right, you tilt onto the right edge. Shifting from left to right is called edge change.

The end of one curve is the beginning of the next. Draw S curves in the snow, not Z's.

What's going on here?

Connected curves
inspire rhythm.
Rhythm permits control.
Jagged corners mean
hard work.

For a carved curve, make the back of the edge follow the same path as the front of the edge.

What's going on here?

The front (tip) of the edge and the back (tail) of the edge pass over the same spot in the snow. When you carve you move through a curve faster than when you skid. The edge grips along a clean line, leaving a narrow groove in the snow.

For a skidded curve, let the back of the edge take a longer path than the front of the edge.

What's going on here?

Skidding is a great way
to slow down. In a
skidding curve, the back
(tail) of the edge is
allowed to break loose.
It takes a longer route
through the curve than
the front (tip) of the edge.
The edge drags along the
snow, helping you brake.
This leaves a broader
track in the snow.

Glide on edge from the curve's beginning...

What's going on here?

An edge skids when it does not grip completely. (Skidding is not always bad. We often want to skid to slow down.) We carve when the edge grips so well we glide through the curve without skidding. Steadily roll the snow toy onto its edge as early as possible in each curve to avoid skidding. The longer you wait to tilt the toy on edge, the harder it is to get good grip and really stay in control.

giving the edge little chance to skid.

Make sure the edge travels outside the path of the body in a curve.

What's going on here?

In most curves, the edge travels a longer distance than you do. Your body takes a shortcut. Align your bones so you can balance against the tipped-up edge. How far your skeleton tilts to the inside depends on how fast you are going.

Support yourself
on your bones...

less on your muscles.

What's going on here?

Your skeleton is what holds you upright, not your muscles. Align your bones so they can support you. This does not mean to ride the snow toy stiff legged but rather to have your joints loosely flexed. If you bend your knees and ankles too much, your muscles will tire more quickly.

Bend the edge to draw a curve.

Bend the edge more
to tighten the curve.

An edge, because it is flexible, will bend naturally when you tip the snow toy on its edge. It flexes under your body weight. Use your muscles to push down on the edge to bend it more. You can bend the edge most toward the end of a curve because you have gravity helping you. (Gravity's pull increases your body weight, making you seem heavier.) The more you bend the edge, the tighter the curve.

Pull, don't push the edge through each curve.

What's going on here?

To have great control of an edge, you must be well balanced on it. You must move your body so it keeps up with the curving edge. If you feel you are pushing the edge through the snow, you are too far back on it. If you feel the edge is beneath or even slightly behind you through the curve, you have control. Get in position to "pull" the edge. It is the difference between being passive through the curve and actively staying ahead of the edge.

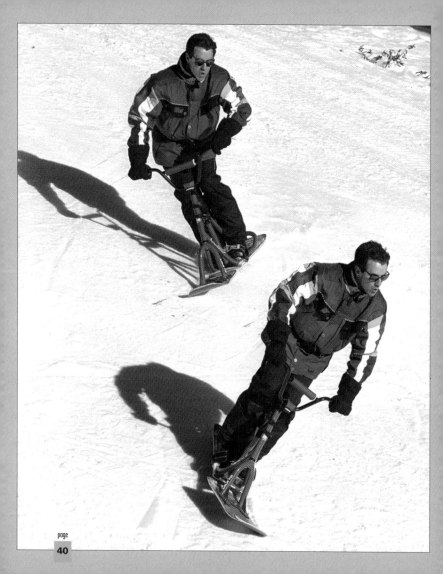

Stay in control by moving away from the hill.

What's going on here?

Leaning toward the hill feels safer and more secure. But to begin a new curve, which helps you stay in control, you have to lean out, away from the hill. By crossing your body over the snow toy—downhill—you automatically change edges.

Shortening...

What's going on here?

When you push down
on an edge to bend it more,
your body shortens. When you
take the pressure off an edge to
let it spring back, your muscles
relax and you seem to get
longer. Because you are gliding
on a slope, the shortening
and lengthening are not so
much down and up movements
as they are closer to the hill
(at the end of one curve) and then
out away from the hill (as you
begin the next curve).

and lengthening the body happen into and away from the hill, not up and down.

Release the stored energy in a bent edge, and it will launch you into the next curve.

What's going on here?

A bent edge is like a spring. When you take the pressure off—as you do without thinking when you change edges—it springs back to its original unbent shape. This moment—when the snow toy unbends—is the time to start your next curve. Using stored-up energy in the snow toy lets your muscles work less.

Chapter 2

Good Things to Know About Gliding on Skis

Skis, the oldest form of over-snow transport, have been around for centuries. During the last 50 years—as down-hill gliding became popular—and especially in the 1990s, skis have become high-tech carving instruments.

Skiing recognizes humans as two-footed creatures, with lower limbs that often work independently. Two skis, of course, provide four working edges. This and the fact that skis come in many lengths, shapes, weights and materials, allow a wide spectrum of speeds and limitless curving possibilities. If ski poles—extensions of the human arm—are also used, skiers become extremely versatile, able to glide on just about any snow-covered terrain.

Legs should be flexing, never locked.

What's going on here?

Stiffness, tension,
and locked joints are
a skier's greatest
enemies. This is
especially true
in the ankles.

Hold your hands ready, where you can see them.

What's going on here?

Your hands are good indicators of what other parts of your body are doing. Lose sight of one hand, and your upper body is probably twisted out of position, not facing where you are going. Your hands must always be ready to touch the ski pole tip to the snow.

Stop your skis from fighting each other...

Match to get them both on the same edge.

What's going on here?

At first you may point your ski tips toward each other to help you brake. This can be unnatural and tiring, because the skis are on different edges. Better to let your skis point in the same direction—and control your speed by curving.

Tip your skis on edge by tilting your leg bones.

What's going on here?

Accurate, powerful curves happen when you tip both legs the way you want to go.

To ski parallel, change both edges of both skis at the same time.

What's going on here?

Lots...but the less
you think about changing
both edges at once,
the easier it is to do.

(See pages 22-23.)

Keep most of your weight on the outside ski.

What's going on here?

More pressure will be
forced toward your
outside ski in every curve.
The faster you go,
and the sharper the curve,
the more pressure you
experience. Encourage
outside-ski pressure, even
exaggerate it when you
really need to grip. If the
outside ski slips out, your
inside leg is there to
help you catch
your balance.

Keep the inside leg out of the way of the outside leg.

What's going on here?

Because your outside leg is doing most of the work, move your inside leg out of the way so the outside leg can do its job. This allows the outside leg to tilt more (see pages 54-55).

Lead with the inside of your body through the curve.

What's going on here?

To let your bones best
support you in a curve
(see pages 34-35), lead
with your inside foot, knee,
and hip. This gives
you better balance
through the curve.

Pole swing and pole plant relate closely to edge change. Quicken your hands to quicken your feet.

What's going on here?

Touching your pole to the snow steadies you as you change edges. Touch the right pole before a curve to the right; touch your left pole before a curve to the left. Since the pole touch is your signal to change edges, the quicker your hands swing the pole tip forward, the more quickly you can link curves (see pages 24-25). This is especially important when you need to make quick turns on a steep slope or in the bumps.

Chapter 3

Good Things to Know
About Gliding on Skiboards

Skiboards are relatively new. They are a cross between mini-skis and skates. Skiboards can be ridden backward as well and forward, and many use them for quick tricks in half-pipes, man-made terrain parks, or on all-mountain terrain. Usually skiboarders use no ski poles, preferring to have their hands free.

Some consider skiboards a stepping stone to skis. New snow gliders adapt to skiboards rapidly, perhaps as quickly as skiers who are used to the security of longer boards. Ski racers and expert skiers often train on skiboards, since they encourage precise balancing movements. Skiboards work best on harder, machine groomed snow surfaces, but become more difficult to ride in softer snow and powder.

Stand on the inside edges of both boards.

Keep tilting both boards on edge through the curve.

What's going on here?

On skis it is important to balance on the edge of the outside ski. On shorter skiboards, it is more stable to stand on the curving edge of both boards. Keep the skiboards on their edges. If you flatten them, they will start to wobble.

Turn your legs more. Move your upper body less.

What's going on here?

In shorter curves, you can throw yourself off balance by turning your upper body too much. Let your legs do the turning. Keep your upper body quiet.

What's going on here?

It is not enough to simply lean
in to ride the blades. Actively stay
ahead of your edges. If you get
behind them, they will scoot out
from under you (see pages 38-39).
Spead your hands apart for balance
and sweep your torso along the
line of the curve.

Lead with your upper body just ahead of the edges.

Chapter 4

Good Things to Know About Gliding on a Snowboard

Snowboards are an on-snow adaptation of surfboards and skateboards. Snowboards have evolved to become highly technical and effective mountain curving tools. A significant percentage of snowgliders make snowboards their toy of choice. They rarely use ski poles.

Both feet are attached to the board itself. Some choose to ride with the left foot forward; others lead with the right. Like skiboards, the snowboard can be ridden forward and backward. A snowboard has a running surface that is much wider than a single ski. This allows it to float comfortably in deeper, softer snow. But it can also be tilted on a very high edge and bent to arc curves. That's why snowboards are also powerful carvers.

Stand equally on both feet to sideslip.

What's going on here ?

Sideslipping is a basic snowboard maneuver. Gripping with the edge behind you (on your heel side), let yourself slip sideways. Play with your weight forward and backward on the board. If you are totally balanced, you will be able to slip straight down the hill. This is a way to get out of tight, steep spots.

To edge on the toe side, push your knees forward to make your shins parallel to the snow.

What's going on here?

On a snowboard, the edge in front of your toes is called the "toe side." The edge behind your heels is called the heel side (see pages 80-81). Note that this rider is standing his left foot foward (this is called "regular" foot). You might stand this way, or you might prefer to stand with your right foot leading (called "goofy" foot). Either stance is correct.

To edge on the heel side, bend your knees as if sitting in a chair.

What's going on here?

A "seated" position lets you push down on the heel side of the snowboard. Keep your ankles flexed. (See next page.) Don't get left behind on a heel side curve. Shift your weight to the front foot at the end of the turn to be ready to start the next turn.

Start a curve with your front leg...

Follow through with your back leg.

What's going on here?

Curving on a snowboard involves a shift of weight from one foot to the other, as well as an edge change. Begin curves with more weight on your front leg. Gradually move your weight toward your back leg to complete the curve.

Actively tip the board with your lower body.

Flow quietly with the upper body.

What's going on here?

It is easy on a snowboard to move too enthusiastically with your upper body and lose your balance. Tilt the board on edge with your feet, legs, and hips, but be more passive with your torso, shoulders, and arms.

Tilt the board on edge to skid.

Tilt it more to carve.

What's going on here?

Remember: a skid is a drifted curve where we try to reduce speed. A carve is a slicing curve, where we make no effort to slow down (see pages 26-29). Either one requires that the board be tipped on edge. It is a matter of how much you edge and how early (see pages 30-31).

Create edge angle by leaning in while staying balanced on the board's edge.

What's going on here?

The amount of edge angle you achieve depends on how much you lean into the curve and bend your legs. Your inside hand can gauge how close you are to the snow.

To ride more aggressively, move the body away from the board, farther inside the curve.

What's going on here?

In a high-speed curve, where the edge is bending and carving, the board should feel like a stable, moving platform you can stand against (see pages 34-35). To withstand the forces in the curve, use your skeleton rather than your muscles. To ride on your bones you may have the sensation that you are moving yourself away from the board as you bank into the curve.

Chapter 5

Good Things to Know About
Gliding on a Snowscoot

The Snowscoot maybe the most powerful snow toy of all. As it evolves it surely offers the greatest possibilities. It is basically a BMX bicycle frame attached to two short snowboards. The scoot's edges slice readily into the hardest, iciest snow, yet the device is extremely stable in difficult conditions.

The Snowscoot is sometimes ridden with both feet pointing forward, sometimes with the feet more sideways, as on a snowboard. Curving scoot riders resemble cornering motorcyclists and motocross riders. It is maneuvered using both the legs and the arms, which partially explains its high-powered performance on snow.

Start by putting your foot on the uphill side first.

What's going on here?

When you first begin, it is easy to get your weight on the wrong edge. When that happens, you and the Snoscoot might tip over. It's best to start out across the hill instead of heading straight down.

Put your other foot on...and go.

Keep both feet on the scoot.

What's going on here?

As you are learning to ride a Snowscoot, you will feel the urge to take your inside foot off to steady yourself. This makes matters worse, since it moves your weight over the wrong edge.

To make a curve, keep some pressure on the front board.

What's going on here?

Get the edge on the scoot's front board to bend and curve by leaning harder on the handlebars

Turn the handlebars to start the curve...

Keep turning the handlebars through the curve.

What's going on here?

The temptation at first is to turn the handlebars, begin a curve, then to stop turning the handlebars. The result is an incomplete curve and too much speed because you are running too straight down the hill.

Control excess skid by turning the handlebars toward the skid.

What's going on here?

It is possible,
especially where it is
steep, that the back
end of the scoot will skid
too much. In this case,
the back of the scoot wants
to become the front.
To avoid this, steer as you
would a skidding car.
Turn the handlebars in
the direction of the skid.

For edge, push down with your inside hand...and inside foot.

What's going on here?

The Snowscoot is a toy that you ride using both your hands and feet. Let your hands and feet work together to control the scoot.

For more edge, pull up with your outside hand.

What's going on here?

You can apply huge leverage to the snow through the handlebars. The more you tilt the handlebars with your arms, and the more you tip the board with your body, the more you'll edge the scoot.

Chapter 6

Good Things to Know About Gliding on a Ski fox

An earlier version of this toy used to be called a "jack-jump." Non-skiing lift operators screwed a 2x4 vertically to an old ski, mounted a seat on top, and rode this device— spectacularly sometimes—to and from their workstations on the mountain. The modern Ski Fox is essentially the same, except for its highly shaped ski and cushy, 21st century suspension developed by a cabinet-maker in Germany.

Light and simple as it looks, the Ski Fox is one of the most thrilling snow toys. Newcomers control it almost immediately, but expertise requires lots of practice miles. Today it is ridden with mini-skis and has tons of built-in turning power. It will carve short curves or long. The Ski Fox defines the idea of gliding on snow by the seat of your pants.

Sit on the seat...
Take the weight
off your feet.

What's going on here ?

Your first impulse may
be to guide the Ski Fox
with your feet. Resist this.
The best way to curve
and control the Fox is
through your butt.

Keep all three skis parallel.

What's going on here ?

On a Ski Fox, you are suddenly a three-legged animal. If one or more of the three skis is allowed to go in a different direction, your feet can get tangled up.

Bend your inside knee.

what's going on here

You will need to keep
your inside leg out of the
way and not put weight
on it (see pages 60-61).

Tilt your body... To skid.

What's going on here ?

Skidding, as you recall,
is about slowing down.
Carving is about maintaining
speed. We need to know
how to do both.

Tilt your seat, but not your body, to carve.

Chapter 7

Good Things to Know About Gliding on a Snowbike

Originally called "skibobs," Snowbikes have been used for decades by seated gliders, mainly in Europe. Newest models are extremely light, efficient, and easy to maneuver. Some can even be immediately disassembled for transport on an aerial tram or gondola lift.

Snowbiking is as exhilarating as any other form of snow gliding, and experts on this toy are as impressive to watch as any world-class skier or snowboarder. What's more, Snowbiking does not require quite the level of physical fitness and conditioning as other snow toys. The seated position, and mini-skis on the rider's feet, offer tremendous control and comfort. If you can ride a bicycle, you can quickly excel on a Snowbike.

Grip the top of the handlebars.

What's going on here ?

Plant your palms
firmly on top of the
handlebars. You will
need to push down on
one side or the other,
using your arms.

Keep weight on the seat...Take weight off the little skis.

What's going on here ?

Again, it is not a good idea to try to guide the Snowbike with your feet.

Hug the seat with your knees.

What's going on here?

You steer the bike
with your thighs and
butt as well as your arms.
Hold your little skis
in close to the bike.

Keep the little skis parallel to the bike's back ski.

what's going on here

Sit tall and far back
on the seat, extend your
arms, and bring your feet
close to the bike's rear ski.
If you ride this way, it's
hard to get your skis
tangled with the bike's.

Turn the handlebars...

What's going on here?

By using the handlebars to gently turn the front ski, and keeping the bike's skis more beneath you, your edges will drag sideways across the snow, slowing you down.

to skid.

Tilt the handlebars...

What's going on here ?

Push down on the
inside handlebar to lever
the bike on its edges early.
This sets up a higher-speed,
carving curve.

To carve.

Push the seat with your outside thigh.

_____

What's going on here ?

As you gain confidence,
you can start to use the
power in your legs.

Chapter 8

Other Good Things to Know

A wise old snow glider once rebuked a newcomer who complained about the mountain weather. "To have good slidin'," he said, "you've got to have nasty weather." Snow is not about palm trees and 80-degree temperatures. The Alpine environment can be harsh, even dangerous to those unaccustomed to cold or wet weather, wind, and intense, high-altitude sunshine. Snowgliding is more fulfilling when you are comfortable—psychologically as well as physically.

Choices you make about how and when you get to the resort, what you wear, how and what you eat, how much liquid you drink, how much you slept the night before, and how body and soul are responding to the experience can turn dreams into nightmares—or vice versa. The key is to know yourself: what you want and what you need.

Dress in layers.

Wearing lots of layers keeps you warmer. It also lets you adjust clothing as the day gets warmer or colder. You can add layers or take some off. The two most important layers are the one closest to your skin and the one on the outside. The best underwear is absorbent enough to "wick" perspiration away from your skin. The outermost layer, including pants, should be wind and water-resistant. Jeans may look cool, but they will get wet—and make you wet—when you fall.

Wear sunscreen.

Most snowgliding takes place at higher altitudes, where the sun's rays are less filtered. Snow also reflects the solar rays, making them even more intense. You can get severely sunburned—very quickly. Wind will burn your skin, too. Even if you have darker skin, or believe you always tan instead of burn, use strong sunscreen anyway. You will be sorry if you don't.

Wear a hat.

You can lose tremendous amounts of body heat through the top of your head. Wear, or at least always carry, a warm hat—even if you hate hats. In addition to a warm hat you

will need a baseball cap or other type of lid to keeps the sun off your face.

Own goggles AND sunglasses.

Infrared and ultraviolet rays can be extremely harmful to your eyes, especially at higher altitudes. Sunglasses—good ones, not cheap ones—are an important investment. Snowblindness, a temporary but serious condition, may result if you forget sunglasses. Wind, cold, fog, and blowing snow can be very uncomfortable to your eyes as well. Goggles are every bit as important as sunglasses. Always take both with you, even if the day seems perfect. Weather changes rapidly in the mountains. It is easy to be caught unprepared.

Memorize a checklist.

A mental checklist, one that you chant to yourself before leaving your home, hotel room, or vehicle, is vital. Check out what experienced skiers might say to themselves before they lock the car door. They hesitate for a few seconds and think, "Skis, boots, poles, hat, gloves, goggles, Chapstick, sunglasses, sunscreen…"

Understand your fitness level.

Snow gliding is for everyone —all ages, all body types, at all degrees of fitness. Be aware, though, that oxygen is less plentiful at higher elevations. It is a little harder to breathe, and you will tire faster. Pace yourself, don't venture too far from resting places and shelter, and don't overdo it. Stay with companions who are close to you in ability and fitness. As you get better on snow toys, you will begin to appreciate how much better you can ride if you get into better shape. In time you may want to consider regular workouts and aerobic training to prepare for snow gliding adventures.

Winterize your car.

Before you travel to a winter sports resort by car, make sure yours is ready for the colder Alpine environment. Check that there is antifreeze in your radiator. Add lightweight winter oil if necessary. You may not be able to justify snow tires, but buy (and carry) a set of tire chains. When it snows heavily, some roads may be closed to all cars without chains or four-wheel drive. It is much cheaper to buy chains near home than it is in the mountains where sellers have you over a barrel. In time, you may want a rooftop rack to carry skis, snowboards, or other snow toys you own. Make sure to zip your car keys into a secure pocket when you go on the mountain. Dozens of keys are lost every day. As a back up, give an extra set of keys to somebody else in your party.

Always wear mittens or gloves.

Some prefer the added warmth of mittens, while others like the finger freedom of gloves. (Some of the newest high-tech gloves are also very warm.) Snowboarders and skiboarders wear extra-thick protection on their hands. It is a mistake to ride any snow toy barehanded, even on warm spring days. The snow surface can be very abrasive to the skin and may leave your hands raw and bloody if you fall.

Eat and sleep well.

You will be happily hungry and tired after a day on snow. You could spoil your afternoon if you eat too heavily at lunch, but eat heartily in the evening. It is especially good to replenish and even "load-up" on carbohydrates. Too much alcohol can make you groggy and dehydrated the next day. Drinking alcohol while skiing is definitely not cool. Your muscles and reactions will be less responsive. A good long night's sleep should make you feel great. Then, as your mother always told you, breakfast is the most important meal of the day. Don't skip breakfast. And take a snack with you in case you run out of gas in the middle of the morning.

Consider a helmet.

Many snowgliders wear helmets. The best ones
are light, comfortable, warm, and allow you to
see and hear clearly. Helmets are cool, as any
kid will tell you. If you use one, you not only provide yourself added protection, you make a fash-
ion statement and don't ever need to worry about
hats. Use a helmet especially designed for snow
gliding, not one meant for another sport.

_____

Warm up and warm down.

Cold weather and high altitudes tend to make our muscles more stiff and sluggish than normal. Allow yourself time to acclimate to the mountain environment before you ride a snow toy. A few warm-up exercises and some stretches you are comfortable with pay big performance dividends. If you stay out in the cold long after you stop exercising, your muscles will stiffen quickly. You can get chilled, even leave yourself vulnerable to a sniffle. Keep moving until you can get inside, take off a few layers, and relax.

Use lip balm.

Chapped lips can be a painful problem. Avoid painful sores and blisters. Carry a tube of lip treatment and use it often. The best lip lubricants also contain sunscreen.

Drink plenty of water.

The atmosphere at higher altitudes tends to be much drier than at sea level. Sun, wind, and your own perspiration conspire to steal your body fluids. In fact, you can become dehydrated long before you even feel thirsty. Stop frequently for water or carry it with you. Coffee, tea, and soda don't replenish your bodily fluids as well as juice or plain water.

Arrive early.

At first, when you don't "know the ropes" at a mountain resort, getting ready and getting out on the mountain seems to take forever. Get to the parking lot early so you don't have to walk—and schlep your stuff—a long way. More rental equipment is available early in the day. Same with snow sports school guides. The snow is generally best in the morning, and lift lines are shortest. It's the best part of the day.

Enjoy!

Snowgliding is exhilarating, but at times it will seem frustrating and exhausting, especially as you try to learn something new or try to move to a higher skill level. Remember: it is all about fun. Other snowgliders may or may not volunteer help, but as a community mountain people are a friendly, helpful lot.  There is always help available—from professional guides and coaches at the snow sports school. The good things they suggest are probably more valuable than advice offered by the Average Joe.